A VINDICATION OF NATURAL DIET

A

VINDICATION

OF

NATURAL DIET

BY

PERCY BYSSHE SHELLY.

A NEW EDITION

"Our simple life wants little, and true tasts
Hires not the pale drudge Luxury to waste
The scene it would adorn, and therefore still
Nature, with all her children, haunts the hill."
Epipsychidion.

KALPAZ

ISBN: 978-93-5128-876-3(PB)

First Published in 1884
Indian Reprint in 2017

Published by

Kalpaz Publications
C-30, Satyawati Nagar,
Delhi – 110052
E-mail: kalpaz@hotmail.com
Website: kalpazpublications.com
Ph.: +91-9212142040

PREFATORY NOTICE.

SHELLEY'S "Vindication of Natural Diet" was first written as part of the notes to "Queen Mab," which was privately issued in 1813. Later in the same year the "Vindication" was separately published as a pamphlet, and it is from this later publication that the present reprint is made. The original pamphlet is now exceedingly scarce, but it is said to have been reprinted in 1835, as an appendix to an American medical work, the "Manual on Health," by Dr. Turnbull, of New York. Two copies only are known to have been preserved of this excessively rare pamphlet, though possibly others may be hidden in unfrequented libraries and out of the way country houses. One copy is in the British Museum, and the other is in the possession of Mr. H. Buxton Forman, who has reprinted it in his great edition of Shelley, where it forms the opening part of the second volume of the "Prose Works."

The main object of Shelley's pamphlet was to show that a vegetable diet is the most *natural*, and therefore the best for mankind. It is not an appeal to humanitarian sentiment, but an argument based on individual experience, concerning the intimate connection of health and morality with food. It has no claim to originality in the arguments adduced; its materials being avowedly drawn from the works of Dr. Lambe and Mr. Newton, of whom an account may be read in Mr. Howard Williams' "Catena," but the style is Shelley's own, and the pamphlet is in many ways one of the most interesting and characteristic of his prose works.

Perhaps its most remarkable feature is to be found in the very pertinent remarks as to the bearing of Vegetarianism on those questions of economy and social reform, which are now forcing themselves more and more on the attention of the English people.*

At the time of writing his "Vindication of Natural Diet," Shelley had himself, for some months past, adopted a Vegetarian diet, chiefly, no doubt, through his intimacy with the Newton family. There seems no reason to doubt that he continued to practise Vegetarianism during the rest of his stay in England, that is from 1813 to the spring of 1818. Leigh Hunt's account of his life at Marlow, in 1817, is as follows:—"This was the round of his daily life. He was up early, breakfasted sparingly, wrote this 'Revolt of Islam' all the morning; went out in his boat, or in the woods, with some Greek author or the Bible in his hands; came home to a dinner of vegetables (for he took neither meat nor wine); visited, if necessary, the sick and fatherless, whom others gave Bibles to and no help; wrote or studied again, or read to his wife and friends the whole evening; took a crust of bread or a glass of whey for his supper, and went early to bed."

In 1818, he left England for Italy, and during his last four years, the most dreamy and speculative period of his life, he seems to have been less strict in his observance of Vegetarian practice. It is not true however, as has sometimes been asserted, that Shelley lost faith in the principles of Vegetarianism; for his change in diet was owing partly to his well-known carelessness about his food, which became more marked at this time, and partly to a desire to avoid

* Shelley's pamphlet appeared in 1813. The Vegetarian Society was not founded until 1847. Information as to this Society, with list of its publications, can be had free on application to the Secretary, 75, Princess Street, Manchester.

giving trouble to the other members of his household, which, as we see from a line in his letter to Maria Gisborne, written in 1820, "Though we eat little flesh and drink no wine" was not entirely a Vegetarian one. Yet, even at this period of his life, he himself was practically, if not systematically, a Vegetarian, for all his biographers agree in informing us that bread was literally his "staff of life." We cannot doubt that if he had lived in the present time he would have taken a leading part in the movement towards Food Reform. As it is, he has left us an invaluable legacy in his "Vindication of Natural Diet," perhaps the most powerful and eloquent plea ever put forward in favour of the Vegetarian cause.

He found in this the presage of his ideal future. To his enthusiastic faith in the transforming effect of the Vegetarian principle, we owe some of the finest passages in his poetry. In the close of the eighth canto of "Queen Mab," we have a picture of a time when man no more

> Slays the lamb that looks him in the face.

It is the same ideal of bloodless innocence as that of Israel's prophet-poet, who declares that in the Holy Mountain they shall not hurt nor destroy. Never did sage or singer, prophet or priest, or poet, see a brighter vision of the future than that which is imaged in the description of a glorified earth, from which cruelty, bloodshed, and tyranny, have been banished.

> "My brethren, we are free! The fruits are glowing
> Beneath the stars, and the night-winds are flowing
> O'er the ripe corn. The birds and beasts are dreaming.
> Never again may blood of bird or beast
> Stain with its venomous stream a human feast,

To the pure skies in accusation steaming;
  Avenging poisons shall have ceased
    To feed disease and fear and madness;
      The dwellers of the earth and air
    Shall throng around our steps in gladness,
      Seeking their food or refuge there.
Our toil from thought all glorious forms shall cull,
To make this earth, our home, more beautiful;
And Science, and her sister Poesy,
Shall clothe in light the fields and cities of the free!"

. . . .

Over the plain the throngs were scattered then
  In groups around the fires, which from the sea
Even to the gorge of the first mountain-glen
  Blazed wide and far. The banquet of the free
  Was spread beneath many a dark cypress-tree;
Beneath whose spires which swayed in the red flame
  Reclining as they ate, of liberty,
And hope, and justice, and Laone's name,
Earth's children did a woof of happy converse frame.

Their feast was such as Earth, the general mother,
  Pours from her fairest bosom, when she smiles
In the embrace of Autumn. To each other
  As when some parent fondly reconciles
  Her warring children, she their wrath beguiles
With her own sustenance; they relenting weep:—
  Such was this festival, which, from their isles
And continents and winds and oceans deep,
All shapes might throng to share that fly or walk or creep.

That this was no mere poetic sentiment is proved by this pamphlet, which is an earnest vindication of Vegetarianism.

H. S. S.
W. E. A. A.

[ORIGINAL TITLE PAGE.]

A

VINDICATION

OF

NATURAL DIET.

BEING ONE IN A SERIES OF NOTES TO QUEEN MAB

(A PHILOSOPHICAL POEM).

Ιαπετιονιδη, παντων περι μηδεα ειδωσ,
Χαιρεισ πυρ κλεψασ, και εμασ φρενασ ηπεροπευσασ;
Σοιτ' αυτω μεγα πημα και ανδρασιν εσσομενοισι.
Τοισδ' έγω αντι πυροσ δωσω κακον, ω κεν απαντεσ
Τερπωνται κατα θυμον, εον κακον αμφαγαπωντεσ.

ΗΣΙΩΔ. Op. et Dies. 1, 54.

LONDON:
PRINTED FOR J. CALLOW, MEDICAL BOOKSELLER, CROWN COURT,
PRINCE'S STREET, SOHO,
BY SMITH & DAVY, QUEEN STREET, SEVEN DIALS.
1813.

PRICE ONE SHILLING AND SIXPENCE.

A VINDICATION OF NATURAL DIET.

I HOLD that the depravity of the physical and moral nature of man originated in his unnatural habits of life. The origin of man, like that of the universe of which he is a part, is enveloped in impenetrable mystery. His generations either had a beginning, or they had not. The weight of evidence in favour of each of these suppositions seems tolerably equal; and it is perfectly unimportant to the present argument which is assumed. The language spoken, however, by the mythology of nearly all religions seems to prove, that at some distant period man forsook the path of nature, and sacrificed the purity and happiness of his being to unnatural appetites. The date of this event seems to have also been that of some great change in the climates of the earth, with which it has an obvious correspondence. The allegory of Adam and Eve eating of the tree of evil, and entailing upon their posterity the wrath of God, and the loss of everlasting life, admits of no other explanation than the disease and crime that have flowed from unnatural diet. Milton was so well aware of this, that he makes Raphael thus exhibit to Adam the consequence of his disobedience :—

> . . . . Immediately a place
> Before his eyes appeared : sad, noisome, dark :
> A lazar-house it seemed ; wherein were laid
> Numbers of all diseased : all maladies
> Of ghastly spasm, or racking torture, qualms
> Of heart-sick agony, all feverous kinds,

Convulsions, epilepsies, fierce catarrhs ;
Intestine stone and ulcer, cholic pangs,
Dæmoniac frenzy, moping melancholy,
And moon-struck madness, pining atrophy,
Marasmus, and wide-wasting pestilence,
Dropsies, and asthmas, and joint-racking rheums.

And how many thousands more might not be added to this frightful catalogue !

The story of Prometheus is one likewise which, although universally admitted to be allegorical, has never been satisfactorily explained. Prometheus stole fire from heaven, and was chained for this crime to Mount Caucasus, where a vulture continually devoured his liver, that grew to meet its hunger. Hesiod says, that, before the time of Prometheus, mankind were exempt from suffering; that they enjoyed a vigorous youth, and that death, when at length it came, approached like sleep, and gently closed their eyes. Again, so general was this opinion, that Horace, a poet of the Augustan age, writes :—

Audax omnia perpeti,
Gens humana ruit per vetitum nefas,
Audax Iapeti genus
Ignem fraude mala gentibus intulit,
Post ignem æthereâ domo
Subductum, macies et nova febrium
Terris incubuit cohors
Semotique prius tarda necessitas
Lethi corripuit gradum.

How plain a language is spoken by all this. Prometheus (who represents the human race) effected some great change in the condition of his nature, and applied fire to culinary purposes; thus inventing an expedient for screening from his disgust the horrors of the shambles. From this moment his vitals were devoured by the vulture of disease. It consumed his being in every shape of its loathsome and infinite variety, inducing the soul-quelling sinkings of premature and violent death. All vice arose from the ruin of healthful innocence. Tyranny, superstitution, commerce, and inequality, were then first known, when reason vainly attempted to guide the wanderings of exacerbated passion. I conclude this part of the subject with an extract from Mr. Newton's Defence of Vegetable Regimen, from whom I have borrowed this interpretation of the fable of Prometheus.

"Making allowance for such transposition of the events of the allegory as time might produce after the important truths were forgotten, which this portion of the ancient mythology was intended to transmit, the drift of the fable seems to be this: Man at his creation was endowed with the gift of perpetual youth; that is, he was not formed to be a sickly suffering creature as we now see him, but to enjoy health, and to sink by slow degrees into the bosom of his parent earth without disease or pain. Prometheus first taught the use of animal food (primus bovem occidit Prometheus)* and of fire, with which to render it more digestible and pleasing to the taste. Jupiter, and the rest of the gods, foreseeing the consequences of these inventions, were amused or irritated at the short-sighted devices of the newly-formed creature, and left him to experience the sad effects of them. Thirst, the necessary concomitant of a flesh diet," (perhaps of all diet vitiated by culinary preparation) "ensued; water was resorted to, and man forfeited the inestimable gift of health which he had received from

*"Plin. Nat. Hist.," Lib. vii., Sec. 57.

heaven; he became diseased, the partaker of a precarious existence and no longer descended slowly to his grave."*

> But just disease to luxury succeeds,
> And every death its own avenger breeds;
> The fury passions from that blood began,
> And turned on man a fiercer savage—Man.

Man and the animals whom he has infected with his society, or depraved by his dominion, are alone diseased. The wild hog, the mouflon, the bison, and the wolf are perfectly exempt from malady, and invariably die either from external violence or natural old age. But the domestic hog, the sheep, the cow, and the dog are subject to an incredible variety of distempers; and, like the corrupters of their nature, have physicians who thrive upon their miseries. The supereminence of man is like Satan's, a supereminence of pain; and the majority of his species, doomed to penury, disease, and crime, have reason to curse the untoward event that, by enabling him to communicate his sensations, raised him above the level of his fellow animals. But the steps that have been taken are irrevocable. The whole of human science is comprised in one question—How can the advantages of intellect and civilisation be reconciled with the liberty and pure pleasures of natural life? How can we take the benefits and reject the evils of the system which is now interwoven with all the fibres of our being? I believe that abstinence from animal food and spirituous liquors would in a great measure capacitate us for the solution of this important question.

Comparative anatomy teaches us that man resembles frugivorous animals in everything, and carnivorous in

* "Return to Nature." Cadell, 1811.

nothing: he has neither claws wherewith to seize his prey, nor distinct and pointed teeth to tear the living fibre. A mandarin of the first class, with nails two inches long, would probably find them alone inefficient to hold even a hare. After every subterfuge of gluttony, the bull must be degraded into the ox, and the ram into the wether, by an unnatural and inhuman operation, that the flaccid fibre may offer a fainter resistance to rebellious nature. It is only by softening and disguising dead flesh by culinary preparation that it is rendered susceptible of mastication or digestion, and that the sight of its bloody juices and raw horror does not excite intolerable loathing and disgust. Let the advocate of animal food force himself to a decisive experiment on its fitness, and, as Plutarch recommends, tear a living lamb with his teeth, and plunging his head into its vitals, slake his thirst with the steaming blood; when fresh from the deed of horror, let him revert to the irresistible instincts of nature that would rise in judgment against it, and say, Nature formed me for such work as this. Then, and then only, would he be consistent.

Man resembles no carnivorous animal. There is no exception, except man be one, to the rule of herbivorous animals having cellulated colons.

The orang-outang perfectly resembles man both in the order and number of his teeth. The orang-outang is the most anthropomorphous of the ape tribe, all of which are strictly frugivorous. There is no other species of animals in which this analogy exists.* In many frugivorous animals, the canine teeth are more pointed and distinct

* Cuvier, Leçons d'Anat. Comp. tom. iii., pages 169, 373, 448, 465, and 480. Rees's Cyclopædia, article Man.

than those of man. The resemblance also of the human stomach to that of the orang-outang is greater than to that of any other animal.

The intestines are also identical with those of herbivorous animals, which present a large surface for absorption, and have ample and cellulated colons. The cæcum also, though short, is larger than that of carnivorous animals; and even here the orang-outang retains its accustomed similarity.

The structure of the human frame then is that of one fitted to a pure vegetable diet, in every essential particular. It is true that the reluctance to abstain from animal food, in those who have been long accustomed to its stimulus, is so great in some persons of weak minds, as to be scarcely overcome; but this is far from bringing any argument in its favour. A lamb which was fed for some time on flesh by a ship's crew, refused its natural diet at the end of the voyage. There are numerous instances of horses, sheep, oxen, and even wood-pigeons, having been taught to live upon flesh, until they have loathed their natural aliment. Young children evidently prefer pastry, oranges, apples, and other fruit, to the flesh of animals, until, by the gradual depravation of the digestive organs, the free use of vegetables has, for a time, produced serious inconveniences; *for a time,* I say, since there never was an instance wherein a change from spirituous liquors and animal food to vegetables and pure water, has failed ultimately to invigorate the body, by rendering its juices bland and consentaneous, and to restore to the mind that cheerfulness and elasticity, which not one in fifty possesses on the present system. A love of strong liquors is also with difficulty taught to infants. Almost every one remembers the wry faces the first glass of port produced. Unsophisticated instinct is invariably unerring; but to decide on the fitness of animal food, from the perverted appetites which its constrained adoption produce, is to make the criminal a judge in his own cause; it is even worse, it is appealing to the infatuated drunkard in a question of the salubrity of brandy.

What is the cause of morbid action in the animal system? Not the air we breathe, for our fellow denizens of nature breathe the same uninjured; not the water we drink, if remote from the pollutions of man and his inventions, for the animals drink it too; not the earth we tread upon; not the unobscured sight of glorious nature, in the wood, the field, or the expanse of sky and ocean; nothing that we are or do in common with the undiseased inhabitants of the forest. Something then wherein we differ from them; our habit of altering our food by fire, so that our appetite is no longer a just criterion for the fitness of its gratification. Except in children there remains no traces of that instinct which determines, in all other animals, what aliment is natural or otherwise; and so perfectly obliterated are they in the reasoning adults of our species, that it has become necessary to urge considerations, drawn from comparative anatomy, to prove that we are naturally frugivorous.

Crime is madness. Madness is disease. Whenever the cause of disease shall be discovered, the root, from which all vice and misery have so long overshadowed the globe, will lie bare to the axe. All the exertions of man, from that moment, may be considered as tending to the clear profit of his species. No sane mind in a sane body resolves upon a real crime. It is a man of violent passions, bloodshot eyes, and swollen veins, that alone can grasp the knife of murder. The system of a simple diet promises no Utopian advantages. It is no mere reform of legislation, whilst the furious passions and evil propensities of the human heart, in which it had its origin, are still unassuaged. It strikes at the root of all evil, and is an experiment which may be tried with success, not alone by nations, but by small societies, families, and even individuals.

In no cases has a return to vegetable diet produced the slightest injury: in most it has been attended with changes undeniably beneficial. Should ever a physician be born with the genius of Locke, I am persuaded that he might trace all bodily and mental derangements to our unnatural habits, as clearly as that philosopher has traced all knowledge to sensation. What prolific sources of disease are not those mineral and vegetable poisons that have been introduced for its extirpation? How many thousands have become murderers and robbers, bigots and domestic tyrants, dissolute and abandoned adventurers, from the use of fermented liquors; who had they slaked their thirst only at the mountain stream, would have lived but to diffuse the happiness of their own unperverted feelings. How many groundless opinions and absurd institutions have not received a general sanction from the sottishness and intemperance of individuals? Who will assert that, had the populace of Paris drank at the pure source of the Seine, and satisfied their hunger at the ever-furnished table of vegetable nature that they would have lent their brutal suffrage to the proscription-list of Robespierre? Could a set of men, whose passions were not perverted by unnatural stimuli, look with coolness on an *auto da fè?* Is it to be believed that a being of gentle feelings, rising from his meal of roots, would take delight in sports of blood?

Was Nero a man of temperate life? Could you read calm health in his cheek, flushed with ungovernable propensities of hatred for the human race? Did Muley Ismael's pulse beat evenly, was his skin transparent, did his eyes beam with healthfulness, and its invariable concomitants, cheerfulness and benignity? Though history has decided none of these questions, a child could not hesitate to answer in the negative. Surely the bile-suffused cheek of Buonaparte, his wrinkled brow, and yellow eye, the ceaseless inquietude of his nervous system, speak no less plainly the character of his unresting ambition than his murders and his victories. It is impossible had Bonaparte descended from a race of vegetable feeders, that he could have either the inclination or the power to ascend the throne of the Bourbons. The desire of tyranny could scarcely be excited in the individual; the power to tyrannise would certainly not be delegated by a society neither frenzied by inebriation, nor rendered impotent or irrational by disease. Pregnant, indeed, with inexhaustible calamity is the renunciation of instinct, as it concerns our physical nature; arithmetic cannot enumerate, nor reason perhaps suspect, the multitudinous sources of disease in civilised life. Even common water, that apparently innoxious *pabulum*, when corrupted by the filth of populous cities, is a deadly and insidious destroyer.* Who can wonder that all the inducements held out by God himself in the Bible to virtue should have been vainer than a nurse's tale; and that those dogmas, apparently favourable to the intolerant and angry passions, should have alone

* See Dr. Lambe's "Report on Cancer."

been deemed essential; whilst Christians are in the daily practice of all those habits which have infected with disease and crime, not only the reprobate sons, but these favoured children of the common Father's love. Omnipotence itself could not save them from the consequences of this original and universal sin.

There is no disease, bodily or mental, which adoption of vegetable diet and pure water has not infallibly mitigated, wherever the experiment has been fairly tried. Debility is gradually converted into strength, disease into healthfulness: madness, in all its hideous variety, from the ravings of the fettered maniac, to the unaccountable irrationalities of ill-temper, that make a hell of domestic life, into a calm and considerable evenness of temper, that alone might offer a certain pledge of the future moral reformation of society. On a natural system of diet, old age would be our last and our only malady: the term of our existence would be protracted; we should enjoy life, and no longer preclude others from the enjoyment of it; all sensational delights would be infinitely more exquisite and perfect; the very sense of being would then be a continued pleasure, such as we now feel it in some few and favoured moments of our youth. By all that is sacred in our hopes for the human race, I conjure those who love happiness and truth, to give a fair trial to the vegetable system. Reasoning is surely superfluous on a subject whose merits an experience of six months would set for ever at rest. But it is only among the enlightened and benevolent that so great a sacrifice of appetite and prejudice can be expected, even though its ultimate excellence should not admit of dispute.

It is found easier, by the short-sighted victims of disease, to palliate their torments by medicine, than to prevent them by regimen. The vulgar of all ranks are invariably sensual and indocile; yet I cannot but feel myself persuaded, that when the benefits of vegetable diet are mathematically proved; when it is as clear, that those who live naturally are exempt from premature death, as that nine is not one, the most sottish of mankind will feel a preference towards a long and tranquil, contrasted with a short and painful life. On the average, out of sixty persons, four die in three years. In April, 1814, a statement will be given that sixty persons, all having lived more than three years on vegetables and pure water, are then *in perfect health.* More than two years have now elapsed; *not one of them has died;* no such example will be found in any sixty persons taken at random. Seventeen persons of all ages (the families of Dr. Lambe and Mr. Newton) have lived for seven years on this diet without a death, and almost without the slightest illness. Surely, when we consider that some of these were infants, and one a martyr to asthma, now nearly subdued, we may challenge any seventeen persons taken at random in this city to exhibit a parallel case. Those who may have been excited to question the rectitude of established habits of diet, by these loose remarks, should consult Mr. Newton's luminous and eloquent essay.* It is from that book, and from the conversation of its excellent and enlightened author, that I have derived the materials which I here present to the public.

* Return to Nature, or Defence of Vegetable Regimen. Cadell, 1811

When these proofs come fairly before the world, and are clearly seen by all who understand arithmetic, it is scarcely possible that abstinence from aliments demonstrably pernicious should not become universal.

In proportion to the number of proselytes, so will be the weight of evidence; and when a thousand persons can be produced, living on vegetables and distilled water, who have to dread no disease but old age, the world will be compelled to regard animal flesh and fermented liquors as slow but certain poison. The change which would be produced by simpler habits on political economy is sufficiently remarkable. The monopolising eater of animal flesh would no longer destroy his constitution by devouring an acre at a meal, and many loaves of bread would cease to contribute to gout, madness, and apoplexy, in the shape of a pint of porter or a dram of gin, when appeasing the long-protracted famine of the hard-working peasant's hungry babes. The quantity of nutritious vegetable matter consumed in fattening the carcase of an ox, would afford ten times the sustenance, undepraving indeed, and incapable of generating disease, if gathered immediately from the bosom of the earth.

The most fertile districts of the habitable globe are now actually cultivated by men for animals, at a delay and waste of aliment absolutely incapable of calculation. It is only the wealthy that can, to any great degree, even now, indulge the unnatural craving for dead flesh, and they pay for the greater licence of the privilege, by subjection to supernumerary diseases. Again, the spirit of the nation that should take the lead in this great reform would insensibly become agricultural: commerce, with all its vice, selfishness, and corruption, would gradually decline; more natural habits would produce gentler manners, and the excessive complication of political relations would be so far simplified that every individual might feel and understand why he loved his country, and took a personal interest in its welfare. How would England, for example, depend on the caprices of foreign rulers, if she contained within herself all the necessaries, and despised whatever they possessed of the luxuries of life? How could they starve her into compliance with their views? Of what consequence would it be that they refused to take her woollen manufactures, when large and fertile tracts of the island ceased to be allotted to the waste of pasturage? On a natural system of diet, we should require no spices from India; no wines from Portugal, Spain, France, or Madeira; none of those multitudinous articles of luxury, for which every corner of the globe is rifled, and which are the causes of so much individual rivalship, such calamitous and sanguinary national disputes.

In the history of modern times, the avarice of commercial monopoly, no less than the ambition of weak and wicked chiefs, seems to have fomented the universal discord, to have added stubbornness to the mistakes of cabinets, and indocility to the infatuation of the people. Let it ever be remembered, that it is the direct influence of commerce to make the interval between the richest and the poorest man wider and more unconquerable. Let it be remembered that it is a foe to every thing of real worth and excellence in the human character. The odious and disgusting aristocracy of wealth, is built upon the ruins of all that is good in chivalry or republicanism; and luxury is the forerunner of a barbarism scarce capable of cure. Is it impossible to realize a state of society, where all the energies of man shall be directed to the production of his solid happiness?

Certainly, if this advantage (the object of all political speculation) be in any degree attainable, it is attainable only by a community which holds out no factitious incentives to the avarice and ambition of the few, and which is internally organized for the liberty, security, and comfort of the many. None must be entrusted with power (and money is the completest species of power) who do not stand pledged to use it exclusively for the general benefit. But the use of animal flesh and fermented liquors, directly militates with this equality of the rights of man. The peasant cannot gratify these fashionable cravings without leaving his family to starve. Without disease and war, those sweeping curtailers of population, pasturage would include a waste too great to be afforded. The labour requisite to support a family is far lighter* than is usually supposed. The peasantry work, not only for themselves, but for the aristocracy, the army, and the manufacturers.

The advantage of a reform in diet is obviously greater than that of any other. It strikes at the root of the evil. To remedy the abuses of legislation, before we annihilate the propensities by which they are produced, is to suppose, that by taking away the effect, the cause will cease to operate. But the efficacy of this system depends entirely on the proselytism of individuals, and grounds its merits, as a benefit to the community, upon the total change of

* It has come under the author's experience that some of the workmen on an embankment in North Wales who, in consequence of the inability of the proprietor to pay them, seldom received their wages, have supported large families by cultivating small spots of sterile ground by moonlight. In the notes to Pratt's Poem, "Bread for the Poor," is an account of an industrious labourer, who by working in a small garden, before and after his day's task, attained to an enviable state of independence.

the dietetic habits in its members. It proceeds securely from a number of particular cases to one that is universal, and has this advantage over the contrary mode, that one error does not invalidate all that has gone before.

Let not too much, however, be expected from this system. The healthiest among us is not exempt from hereditary disease. The most symmetrical, athletic, and long-lived, is a being inexpressibly inferior to what he would have been, had not the unnatural habits of his ancestors accumulated for him a certain portion of malady and deformity. In the most perfect specimen of civilized man something is still found wanting by the physiological critic. Can a return to nature, then, instantaneously eradicate predispositions that have been slowly taking root in the silence of innumerable ages? Indubitably not. All that I contend for is, that from the moment of the relinquishing all unnatural habits, no new disease is generated; and that the predisposition to hereditary maladies gradually perishes for want of its accustomed supply. In cases of consumption, cancer, gout, asthma, and scrofula, such is the invariable tendency of a diet of vegetables and pure water.

Those who may be induced by these remarks to give the vegetable system a fair trial, should, in the first place, date the commencement of their practice from the moment of their conviction. All depends upon the breaking through a pernicious habit resolutely and at once. Dr. Trotter* asserts that no drunkard was ever reformed by gradually relinquishing his dram. Animal flesh, in its effects on the human stomach, is analogous to a dram. It is similar in

* See Trotter on "The Nervous Temperament."

the kind, though differing in the degree, of its operation. The proselyte to a pure diet must be warned to expect a temporary diminution of muscular strength. The subtraction of a powerful stimulus will suffice to account for this event. But it is only temporary, and is succeeded by an equable capability for exertion far surpassing his former various and fluctuating strength. Above all, he will acquire an easiness of breathing, by which the same exertion is performed with a remarkable exemption from that painful and difficult panting now felt by almost every one after hastily climbing an ordinary mountain. He will be equally capable of bodily exertion or mental application after as before his simple meal. He will feel none of the narcotic effects of ordinary diet. Irritability, the direct consequence of exhausting stimuli, would yield to the power of natural and tranquil impulses. He will no longer pine under the lethargy of *ennui*, that unconquerable weariness of life, more dreaded than death itself. He will escape the epidemic madness that broods over its own injurious notions of the Deity, and "realizes the hell that priests and beldams feign." Every man forms, as it were, his god from his own character; to the divinity of one of simple habits, no offering would be more acceptable than the happiness of his creatures. He would be incapable of hating or persecuting others for the love of God. He will find, moreover, a system of simple diet to be a system of perfect epicurism. He will no longer be incessantly occupied in blunting and destroying those organs from which he expects his gratification. The pleasures of taste to be derived from a dinner of potatoes, beans, peas, turnips, lettuces, with a dessert of apples, gooseberries, strawberries, currants, raspberries, and in winter, oranges, apples, and pears, is far greater than is supposed. Those who wait until they can eat this plain fare with the sauce of appetite will scarcely join with the hypocritical sensualist at a lord mayor's feast, who declaims against the pleasures of the table. Solomon kept a thousand concubines, and owned in despair that all was vanity. The man whose happiness is constituted by the society of one amiable woman would find some difficulty in sympathising with the disappointment of this venerable debauchee.

I address myself not only to the young enthusiast, the ardent devotee of truth and virtue, the pure and passionate moralist, yet unvitiated by the contagion of the world. He will embrace a pure system, from its abstract truth, its beauty, its simplicity and its promise of wide-extended benefit; unless custom has turned poison into food, he will hate the brutal pleasures of the chase by instinct; it will be a contemplation full of horror and disappointment to his mind, that beings capable of the gentlest and most admirable sympathies, should take delight in the death-pangs and last convulsions of dying animals. The elderly man whose youth has been poisoned by intemperance, or who has lived with apparent moderation, and is afflicted with a variety of painful maladies, would find his account in a beneficial change, produced without the risk of poisonous medicines. *The mother, to whom the perpetual restless-

*See Mr. Newton's book. His children are the most beautiful and healthy creatures it is possible to conceive; the girls are perfect models for a sculptor: their dispositions are also the most gentle and conciliating; the judicious treatment which they experience in other points, may be a correlative cause of this. In the first five years of their life, of 18,000 children that are born, 7,500 die of various diseases; and how many more of those that survive are rendered miserable by maladies not immediately mortal? The quality and quantity of a woman's milk are materially injured by the use of dead flesh. In an island, near Iceland, where no vegetables are to be got, the children invariably die of tetanus, before they are three weeks old, and the population is supplied from the mainland.—*Sir G. Mackenzie's History of Iceland.* See also *Emile*, chap. i., p. 53, 55, 56.

ness of disease, and unaccountable deaths incident to her children, are the causes of incurable unhappiness, would on this diet experience the satisfaction of beholding their perpetual health and natural playfulness.

The most valuable lives are daily destroyed by diseases, that it is dangerous to palliate and impossible to cure by medicine. How much longer will man continue to pimp for the gluttony of death, his most insidious, implacable, and eternal foe? The proselyte to a simple and natural diet, who desires health, must from the moment of his conversion attend to these rules—

> NEVER TAKE ANY SUBSTANCE INTO THE STOMACH THAT ONCE HAD LIFE.

> DRINK NO LIQUID BUT WATER RESTORED TO ITS ORIGINAL PURITY BY DISTILLATION.

APPENDIX.

Persons on vegetable diet have been remarkable for longevity. The first Christians practised abstinence from animal flesh, on a principle of self mortification. Other instances are, Old Parr 152; Mary Patten 136; A Shepherd in Hungary 126; Patrick O'Neale 113; Joseph Elkins 103; Elizabeth de Val 101; Aurungzebe 100; St. Anthony 105; James, the Hermit 104; Arsenius 120; St. Epiphanius 115; Simeon 112; and Rombald 120.

Mr. Newton's mode of reasoning on longevity is ingenious and conclusive. "Old Parr, healthy as the wild animals, attained to the age of 152 years. All men might be as healthy as the wild animals. Therefore all men might attain to the age of 152 years." The conclusion is sufficiently modest. Old Parr cannot be supposed to have escaped the inheritance of disease, amassed by the unnatural habits of his ancestors. The term of human life may be expected to be infinitely greater, taking into the consideration all the circumstances that must have contributed to abridge even that of Parr.

It may be here remarked, that the author and his wife have lived on vegetables for eight months. The improvements of health and temper here stated, is the result of his own experience.

ESSAYS ON DIET,

BEING

Collected Lectures and Papers on Vegetarian Diet.

By FRANCIS WILLIAM NEWMAN.

LONDON: KEGAN PAUL, TRENCH, AND CO.; AND THE VEGETARIAN SOCIETY, 75, PRINCESS STREET, MANCHESTER.

PRICE ONE FLORIN.

THE

PERFECT WAY IN DIET:

A TREATISE ADVOCATING A RETURN TO THE NATURAL AND ANCIENT FOOD OF OUR RACE.

By ANNA KINGSFORD,

Doctor of Medicine of the Faculty of Paris.

London : Kegan Paul, Trench, and Co., 1, Paternoster Square; or from the Vegetarian Society, 75, Princess Street, Manchester.

PRICE ONE FLORIN.

Price 6d. 64pp., 8vo. Post free, 7d.

"ALMONDS AND RAISINS" FOR 1884.

Edited by R. BAILEY WALKER, F.S.S.

CONTAINS :—

Mushrooms and Toadstools. By H. S. S.
A Hunting of the Deer. By E. Dudley Warner.
A Christmas Ghost. By E. Grenville Waller.
The Ribblesdalo Papers—Nos. I.-IV. By "Dora."
Rubies from Ruskin.
The Ministry of Food. By R. Bailey Walker.
The Abbot's Reply. By W. E. A. Axon.
Almonds and Raisins. By E. J. Baillie.
The Torquoise Ring. A Story by Mrs. Anna Kingsford, M.D.
Kalendar and Notes for 1884.
Fruits in Season for each Month, &c., &c.

75, Princess Street, Manchester.

THE SHELLEY SOCIETY

PUBLICATIONS FOR 1886

THE SHELLEY SOCIETY

PUBLICATIONS FOR 1886.

The Society's Publications for 1886 will be at least twelve of the following fourteen:—

1. Shelley's *Adonais:* an Elegy on the Death of John Keats. Pisa, 4to, 1821. A Facsimile Reprint on hand-made Paper, edited, with a Bibliographical Introduction, by Thomas J. Wise. (*Second Edition, Revised.*) 10*s.* [*Issued.*

2. Shelley's Review of Hogg's novel, "Memoirs of Prince Alexy Haimatoff." Now first reprinted from *The Critical Review*, Dec. 1814, on hand-made Paper, with an Extract from Prof. Dowden's article, "Some Early Writings of Shelley" (*Contemp. Rev.*, Sept. 1884). Edited, with an Introductory Note, by Thos. J. Wise. (*Second Edition, Revised.*) 2*s.* 6*d.* [*Issued.*

3. Shelley's *Alastor*, or The Spirit of Solitude; and other Poems. London, fcap. 8vo., 1816. A Facsimile Reprint on hand-made Paper, with a new Preface by Bertram Dobell. (*Second Edition, Revised.*) 6*s.* [*Issued.*

4. *A Shelley Bibliography*, or "The Shelley Library." Part I. First Editions and their Reproductions. By H. Buxton Forman. [*Issued.*

5. Shelley's *Vindication of Natural Diet.* London, 12mo, 1813. A Reprint, 1882, with a Prefatory Note by H. S. Salt and W. E. A. Axon. Presented by Mr. Axon. (*Second Edition.*) [*Issued.*

6. *A Memoir of Shelley*, with a fresh Preface, by William Michael Rossetti; a Portrait of Shelley; and an engraving of his Tomb. [*Issued.*

7. Shelley's *Cenci*, (for the Society's performance in May), with a prologue by Dr. John Todhunter, and an Introduction and Notes by Harry Buxton Forman and Alfred Forman; and a Portrait of Beatrice Cenci. 2*s.* 6*d.* [*Issued.*